Purposeful

LIVING IN GOD'S DIVINE PURPOSE!

Nikeya P. Quick

REJOICE
Essential Publishing

Author's website: www.nikeyaquickministries.com

Purposeful/ Nikeya P. Quick

ISBN-13: 978-1-956775-89-1

Dedication

I DEDICATE THIS BOOK TO my three children, Alexander, Cameron, and Brandon. I love you immensely. I am grateful to be your mother. You were included in the purpose and will of God concerning my life.

Table of Contents

ACKNOWLEDGEMENTS.....................................vii

FOREWORD...viii

INTRODUCTION...1

CHAPTER 1: God's Creation.............................6

CHAPTER 2: The Purpose of Jesus Christ....10

CHAPTER 3: The Purpose of the Believer.....17

CHAPTER 4: God's Anointing for Your
                    Purpose..23

CHAPTER 5: Grace for Your Purpose............29

CHAPTER 6: Staying Connected to the
                    Vine...33

CHAPTER 7: Discerning Times and
                    Seasons.......................................38

ABOUT THE AUTHOR...................................47

REFERENCES...49

Acknowledgements

I WANT TO ACKNOWLEDGE GOD the Father, Jesus Christ, my Lord and Savior, and the Holy Spirit for helping me fulfill the purpose and plan of God concerning my life.

I want to acknowledge my Pastors, Apostle Sam and Dr. Rico Wagner for their love and support and for being an example of fulfilling the purpose and plan of God. I thank you for your encouragement and for teaching the Word of God in such an impactful and balanced manner. Thank you for your vision and affirmations. Thank you for seeing me the way that God views me. With Love. — *Nikeya Q.*

Foreword

*I*T'S MY HONOR AND privilege to write the foreword for this ground-breaking faith-filled book on living a purpose-driven life.

God planned your life and uniquely designed you perfectly to fulfill His purposes. Every aspect of your life—including your physical features, personality, parents, and so on—is a gift. You can't repay God for all He's given you, but you can express your gratitude by fulfilling God's purpose for your life.

This book is a beacon of hope, guiding us toward a life of purpose and fulfillment. It encapsulates the desire to live a life driven by God's plans, a life that is not just about existing, but about experiencing joy in every step of the journey.

There's nothing more disheartening than waking up each day feeling like a ship without a rudder. You look around and see others, your friends and coworkers, living lives filled with passion, meaning, and direction. They seem to have it all figured out, and you can't help but wonder, 'What about me?'

You know that God has something good in store just for you. You don't believe He intends you to live a life of painful drudgery in which each day is a total drag. After all, the Bible is full of passages about joy and purpose. While this certainly doesn't mean that every day is a parade, it does mean that an overall sense of gladness should permeate your life.

In *Psalm 63:7, David said, "...for you have been my help, and in the shadow of your wings I will sing for joy."* How can you get to that place? Instead of wandering aimlessly through life, you're actually singing for joy (or just making a joyful noise if you're not the singing type).

In this book, Nikeya P. Quick addresses points that you may not be living in the fullness of God's purpose for you. We have a purpose for how to begin living a meaningful, enthusiastic, purpose-filled life and experience joy in the process.

Dr. Rico Wagner
New Foundation Church International

I've written several forewords in my life, and I'm honored to have been asked to do so. I'm honored to write this foreword for *"Purposeful"* by Nikeya Quick, a faithful member and evangelist of *New Foundation Church International.* I know this one is going to be filled with divine revelations and experiences from Nikeya's life. The apostle Paul wrote, *And know that all things work together for good to those who love God, to those who are the called according to His purpose (Romans 8:28 NKJV).*

To me, Nikeya Quick writes like Apostle Paul. Both have seen something and touched something that will develop our understanding according to God's purpose. In this book, Nikeya speaks of the things she's observed in worship, studying the Word, preaching, and evangelism from a personal encounter with the Word of God. These are things that will make a believer walk by faith and not by sight. This book calls us to look into the Word to develop our close relationship with the Lord and help us to know the mind of Christ.

God expects us to know our purpose, considering he was the one who defined it according to *Jeremiah 29:11: For I know the thoughts that I think toward you, says the Lord, thoughts of peace and not of evil, to give you a future and a hope.* I believe this book will be a guide to help you understand God's will, which is His purpose, and our roles in the church, home, and family. Surely as I live, says the Lord, all of the earth shall be filled with the glory of the Lord.

Nikeya will help you step by step to understand your God-given purpose so you can experience the fullness of His blessings and a plan that only He can help you fulfill in his earthen vessel.

Apostle Sam Wagner
New Foundation Church International

Introduction

2 TIMOTHY 1:9 NIV, "HE has saved us and called us to a holy life-not because of anything we have done but because of his own purpose and grace. This grace was given us in Christ Jesus before the beginning of time."

Living a life full of purpose and meaning is something that every human being desires. The thought of being a failure in life or not having any meaning for being here can and will cause us to become hopeless.

Not having a reason for simply existing can become exhausting and mundane. The different stages of our lives that we go through as human beings, requires us to live with a purpose.

Happiness comes from within. It is the inner man of a person that is filled with the purpose that God has originally created us to fulfil. Without this in action, we will be disappointed and empty.

Knowing your purpose is when you can do something that comes naturally to you and also brings fulfillment and a change in the earth that you and others can benefit from. This is my personal description of what purpose feels like.

According to the *"Greater Good Science Center at the University of California, Berkeley,"* purpose is all about applying your skill toward contributing to the greater good in a way that matters to you. The overall perspective of the writer states that you must be able to *"sequentially:"*

- identify the things you care about
- reflect on what matters most, recognize your strengths and talents
- try volunteering
- imagine your best possible self
- cultivate positive emotions like gratitude and awe

- look to people you admire

I recently did a live video on social media to encourage others in Christ. Afterwards, a friend from high school reached out to me and asked me, *"How did you find your purpose in life?"* As he watched my video, he identified that I had found my purpose.

It wasn't until after I received salvation and gave my life to Jesus Christ that I started understanding and learning my purpose. These were things I weren't doing before. In the present, I end up going places and being in the right place at the right time to help someone either with the knowledge I had obtained, helping them physically, monetarily, preaching salvation to them, or even praying for them. It was then that I learned that not only was my purpose to be a wife, a mother, a daughter, a sister, and an aunt but that I am an intercessor, that I am called to evangelize, I am a leader, I am an administrator, and that I was a praise dancer. I showed signs of all these things in my childhood and youth, but I had no clue what they were.

I didn't have the desire to please God, be a believer in Jesus Christ, walk by faith, be a better person, impact others, bring change in the earth, establish biblical views or perspectives, show meaningful kindness and compassion, help bring others into salvation, spread the gospel of Jesus Christ, to be light and salt in the earth, allow my parenting skills to be my ministry at home, allow my life to minister to my family, to be an encourager, an uplifter, a strong support to others, or to be a positive example of overcoming obstacles and embracing change. All these things began to come to me after I received salvation.

This book will enlighten you and help you identify your purpose so you can walk in it by faith in Jesus Christ!

Prayer:

Heavenly Father, I pray that you will begin to shine your light in my life so that I will learn and know my purpose here in the earth. I want to fulfill your purpose for my life, so that you and you alone will get the glory out of my life. I surrender my all to you. I ask you to take control of my life. In Jesus' name. Amen.

CHAPTER 1

God's Creation

*E*VERY HUMAN BEING IS created in the image and likeness of God. *Genesis 1:26-27* proves that we are all God's creation.

> *Genesis 1:26, And God said,*
> - *let us make man in our image,*
> - *after our likeness:*
> - *and let them have dominion over the fish of the sea*
> - *and over the fowl of the air,*
> - *and over the cattle,*
> - *and over all the earth,*
> - *and over every creeping thing that creepeth upon the earth,*

Genesis 1:27 says, "So God created man in his own image, in the image of God created he him; male and female created he them."

God is such a generous God! The Bible lets us know that *the earth is the Lord's and everything in it, the world and all its people belong to him (Psalms 24:1)*. I love how our God is a giving God. He created the earth for His purpose. Nothing that God creates comes without a purpose. Have you ever looked at the most horrendous bug, animal, or plant and thought, *"Why would God create that?"* To us as human beings, if something doesn't look pleasing to us or can't benefit us in a positive way, we may see no purpose for it. God created everything in the earth with us in mind.

After God created male and female, He begins to explain our purpose for being placed in the earth. This is explained in *Genesis 1:28: And God blessed them, and God said unto them,*

- *Be fruitful,*
- *and multiply,*
- *and replenish the earth,*

- *and subdue it:*
- *and have dominion over the fish of the sea,*
- *and over the fowl of the air,*
- *and over every living thing that moves upon the earth.*

Our corporate purpose as human beings has been given to us but we also are given an individual purpose as well. Afterwards the Lord gave us instructions to go along with our corporate purpose. This is explained in *Genesis 1:29,* which reads: And God said,

- *Behold I have given you every herb bearing seed, which is upon the earth,*
- *and every tree, in the which is the fruit of the tree yielding seed;*
- *to you it shall be for meat*
- *and to every beast of the earth,*
- *and to every fowl of the air*
- *and to everything that creepeth upon the earth wherein there is life, I have given every green herb for meat, and it was so.*

God's purpose and plan for humanity overall cannot be explained any clearer than this. We have each been designed to bring glory to the Almighty God. As I meditate on these scriptures, it makes me examine my own life. Even though I have an individual purpose, am I fulfilling my purpose as a human being? Am I walking in dominion over the things He said I can? Am I fruitful? Have I multiplied? Have I replenished the earth and subdued it?

This is something to really think about. Our efforts could be in vain if we are not fulfilling the purpose that God has created for us.

Prayer:

Heavenly Father, I thank you for being my creator and creating for your purpose. Lord, if I am not living out my God-given purpose, I pray that you will reveal to me the areas of my life where I need to submit myself to you, so that your purpose is fulfilled in my life. Captivate my heart and my mind with your will. In Jesus' name. Amen.

CHAPTER 2

The Purpose of Jesus Christ

*J*ESUS CHRIST GIVES US the perfect example of fulfilling the purpose for humanity and our individual purpose.

John 1:1-4 explains who Jesus Christ is, *He is the Word. He was with God and the Word was God. The same was in the beginning with God. All things were made by Him, and nothing was made without Him. In Him was life; and the life was the light of men.*

Jesus Christ was created to bring life to men. I love studying the books of the Gospel of Jesus Christ because you get to hear Jesus tell you what His purpose was. He was so sure of His purpose that no matter who or what opposed it, He would still state the facts of it and still do it.

How many of us can say that we don't get discouraged, frustrated, or even quit walking in our purpose when we face opposition? We lose hope when others don't believe in us. We isolate ourselves and take on a victim mentality. Nowadays, we call people who don't know who we are, see our purpose or does not affirm us, *"our haters."* Jesus was only affirmed by God, when He was baptized by John the Baptist and the Holy Spirit descended upon Him as a dove and God spoke audibly, *"This is my beloved son, in whom I am well pleased!"* Even His disciples didn't know who He was when He asked them. The Jews, who were His own people, weren't sure of who He was. John the Baptist began his ministry by announcing the coming of Jesus Christ, but at the end of his ministry, he was unsure. Jesus never let other people's thoughts about Him stop Him from fulfilling His purpose.

There are so many slogans going on. The one that bothers me the most is *"Prove them Wrong!"*

The only person we must prove wrong is the devil. He is the number one opposer to our purpose. The only person we must please is God by doing His will, which is his purpose for our lives. We will always be able to find God's will for our lives in His Word.

Jesus is my hero, simply because of the way He handled so many situations that He faced. I want to be just like Him in the face of adversity. His purpose was opposed through temptation, persecution, jealousy, envy, accusations, lies, betrayal, and mockery. Jesus was even called Beelzebub, which means the devil. Although He faced those things, he walked in His purpose and stayed the course. Men would glorify God because of His obedience and willingness to God. We can only fulfill our purpose if we are willing and obedient, no matter what it looks like.

When the devil tempted Jesus after He fasted 40 days and 40 nights in the wilderness, he was trying to destroy His purpose. He asked Jesus to make a stone into bread, even though Jesus was living by the Word that came from God's mouth. He asked Jesus to throw himself down to see if God would save him, which was tempting God. He lastly asked Jesus to fall and worship him so that he could give him all the kingdoms of the earth, even though they already belonged to him. Jesus stood on the Word of God and the devil left Him alone. If Jesus would have given in to anything the devil asked him to do, He would not have fulfilled God's purpose for humanity, as being his only Begotten Son. Jesus was submitted to God in every area of his life. The Bible instructs us to submit yourselves therefore to God. *Resist the devil and he will flee from you. —James 4:7*

1 John 3:8 states the purpose of Jesus Christ: *For this purpose, the son of God was manifested, that he might destroy the works of the devil.*

Jesus was hated by the religious leaders, such as the Scribes, Pharisees, Sadducees, and High Priests because He ministered to the people freely, without any restraints or the keeping of the law. The law said touch not, taste not, handle not, but because Jesus Christ came full of grace and truth, He did not keep the law. As He walked in the earth, He fulfilled the law so that we could live by His grace and truth. They thought that Jesus broke the law by letting His disciples eat corn on the sabbath, by healing the sick on the sabbath, and by casting out demons. People hated Him because He healed the sick, opened blind eyes, caused the deaf to hear, the dumb to speak, and the lame to walk, raised the dead, made those whom He healed whole and cast out demons. All of the things Jesus did, destroyed the works of the devil!

The miracles Jesus performed improved people's quality of life. All these things we have named give life to people and set them free.

Jesus made it known that He did not come to abolish the law, but to fulfill it and the prophets. As He did that, He gave us two laws that we must keep:

- *Love the Lord your God, with all your heart, soul and mind*
- *Love your neighbor as yourself*

On these two commandments hang all the law and the prophets. —Matthew 21: 37-40.

In every stage of Jesus's assignment, He knew His purpose even up until His death. When Jesus knew that Judas would betray him, He stated the purpose of His betrayal. When the time came for His betrayal, He prepared for it by praying in the garden of Gethsemane with His disciples. As horrible of a death He faced, He cried out to God to take the cup from Him, but he surrendered to the will of God, which was His purpose. When they scourged Him, mocked Him, spit on Him, made false accusations against Him, beat him, placed the crown of thorns on Him, and crucified Him, He stated His purpose. Before Jesus took His last breath on the cross, He said, *"It is finished!"* Jesus Christ was obedient even to His death.

Some of our purpose will cost us. We will have to leave some people, places, and things behind because they don't fit into our purpose. Jesus had to leave His mother, brother, and sister to fulfill His purpose. He let the disciples know that, only He that does the will of the Father are His mother, sister, and brothers. He continued to minister to the people, heal the sick and cast out demons. No one on earth can do what Jesus did and it have the effect on humanity that it does. Only the blood of Jesus Christ is enough to suffice for the sins of man.

Jesus's birth, crucifixion, death, burial, resurrection, ascension, being crowned as the King of King and Lord of Lords, and becoming our chief intercessor fulfilled God's Purpose for his life.

Prayer:

Heavenly Father, I thank you for the example that your only begotten Son, Jesus Christ, gave us as He walked in the earth. I pray that even as He fulfilled His purpose in the earth, that I too will fulfil my purpose. I ask that you lead and guide me in the way that I should go. I will deny myself, my will, my wants, and my desires so that you will be pleased with me in this life and the life to come in Jesus' name. Amen.

CHAPTER 3

The Purpose of the Believer

*I*N JEREMIAH 1:5, GOD told *Jeremiah that He knew him before He formed him in his mother's womb, and that He had set him apart. He had appointed Jeremiah as a prophet to the nations.* This scripture is proof that each person's purpose is formed inside of them before they are in their mother's womb. God already prepared us to know and do His purpose. It is up to us as individuals to know, live and be what we were purposed for.

According to the Oxford English Dictionary, purpose is a noun defined as *"the reason for which something is done or created or for which something exists; the result or effect intended or sought; the end to which an object or action..."*

In the Strong's Concordance, the word purpose is Hebrew, reference #H2656: "hepes", defined as:

- delight, pleasure
- desire, longing
- good pleasure
- that in which one takes delight
- acceptable
- willingly

As I reviewed the definition of pleasure according to the Word of God, we should find pleasure in our purpose. God never intended for any of our lives to be dreadful or unfulfilling. To live a life full of His purpose, we must seek Him for this, and He will then reveal it to us.

As the Lord revealed Jeremiah's purpose to Him, it brought delight to the Lord and Jeremiah.

Our purpose is often revealed through our gifts, talents, and abilities. We show signs of our purpose as early as being a baby, a child, and adolescence. God has given to humanity so many gifts and talents that they are unable to be numbered.

I am immediately taken to *Romans 11:29 NIV, which reads, "for God's gifts and call are irrevocable."* This means that everything that God has given to us He does not take them back from us. We must learn to embrace the giftings that He has given us and learn how to use them for his glory.

As the definition states *"that in one which takes delight,"* God's gifting within us, will bring delight to us and Him.

When Jesus ascended into heaven, He led captivity captive, and gave gifts to men. The gifts that He gave to men were some:
- *apostles*
- *prophets*
- *evangelists*
- *pastors*
- *teachers*

The purpose of these gifts is to perfect the saints, for the work of the ministry, for the edify-

ing of the body of Christ (Ephesians 4:8-12). As we continue to read about the gifts of God, in *1 Corinthians 12:28*, the Apostle Paul is explaining to the Corinthians about who God has set in the church. He names them as:

- *first apostles*
- *secondarily, prophets*
- *thirdly teachers*
- *after that miracles*
- *then the gift of healings*
- *helps*
- *governments*
- *diversity of tongues*

this explains the hierarchy of the gifts. Earlier in that chapter, *1 Corinthians 12:4-11, There are different kinds of gifts, but the same Spirit distributes them. There are different kinds of service, but the same Lord. There are different kinds of working, but in all of them and in everyone it is the same God at work, now to each one the manifestation of the Spirit is given for the common good.*

- *Word of wisdom*
- *Word of knowledge*
- *Faith*
- *Gift of healing*

- *Working of miracles*
- *Prophecy*
- *Discerning of spirits*
- *Divers kinds of tongues*
- *Interpretation of tongues*

All these are the work of one and the same Spirit, and He distributes them to each one, just as He determines.

God knows our purpose and gives us gifts that align with the purpose that He has assigned to us. This is the perfect reason for us to keep jealousy, envy, covetousness, competition, and comparison away from us. We should not covet a gifting no matter how great or what hierarchy it is named according to the Word of God. The Bible tells us that we should covet prophesy because the Lord wishes that all would prophesy. Prophesy edifies people. It brings exhortation, exaltation, and comfort.

We cannot operate outside of the measure of faith that has been given to us each individually as we operate in these giftings. The Bible also tells us not to class ourselves, with those who compare themselves against others, because they are not wise. Comparison will cause us to operate in pride, make us feel inefficient, ineffective, and overall, not fulfill our purpose, which is to do the will of God. Jesus did not compete with the high priests, rulers, Sadducees, Pharisees, and scribes. He stayed focused on the will and purpose of God assigned to Him. We must do the same. Jesus operated in every gift and calling named Ephesians 4 and 1 Corinthians 12 during His time here in the earth. He is the walking, talking, and living Word.

Prayer:

Heavenly Father, I thank you for the gifts that you have placed inside of me, for you to use for your glory. I dedicate that giftings that you have given to me, to you. I want you to be pleased with what I do with what you have given me. Lord, give me fresh insight so that I may operate in the capacity and measure of faith that you have given me to do your will and fulfill your purpose in Jesus' name. Amen.

CHAPTER 4

God's Anointing For Your Purpose

*Y*OUR PURPOSE WILL ALWAYS be consistent with the Word of God. According to the Cambridge Dictionary, the English meaning of *"consistent"* is to agree with something said or done previously. In the earlier chapters, we learned that God knew us and placed His purpose in us before we were formed in our mother's womb. This establishes the truth of your purpose and that it is consistent with His Word.

We know God's thoughts and intentions towards us are good and not evil, and He wants to give us an end that we expect (Jeremiah 29:11).

As we search through the Bible, from the beginning to the end, from the Old Testament to the New Testament, we see the unveiling of purpose in the lives of those who were called by God.

King David is a great example of God's purpose being consistent with his word concerning his life. David displayed attributes of a king early on in life. He was a shepherd boy, caring for his father's sheep, protecting them, feeding them, leading them to clean pastures, and leading them beside the still waters for them to drink and be restored. This was a defining moment in David's life. He was faithful over something as small as shepherding and was able to lead God's people.

A king that has been appointed by God has to be able to *rule with righteousness, justice, and mercy and truth will go before his face (Psalms 89:10).* During David's tenure as a Shepherd, he had to learn when to give justice to his sheep.

He killed a lion and a bear with his bare hands to defend the sheep he was watching over. He had to know how to navigate the fields and know which fields were good for the sheep to graze in. He had to know the terrain and where the clean water was. David knew when the sheep were hungry, thirsty, tired, and ready to travel. He was willing to endure with the sheep to ensure they were okay.

David is described as *"a man after God's own heart"* when Saul's kingship was being dismantled because of his disobedience to God.

"But now your kingdom shall not endure. The Lord has sought out for Himself a man (David) after His own heart, and the Lord has appointed him as leader and ruler over His people, because you have not kept (obeyed) what the Lord commanded you." —1 Samuel 13:14,

When the Lord sent Samuel to anoint David, Samuel tried to pour the oil over 6 of Jesse's sons prior to him asking the father if there was another. When Jesse called for David, and Samuel saw Jesse the Lord told him to "arise and anoint him, for this is he" After he was anointed, the Spirit of the Lord came upon David from that day forward.

God gives you everything you need to fulfill His purpose for your life! David wouldn't be able to be the King that God created him to be without His anointing.

Your purpose comes with God's anointing. This is why we must ensure that we are operating in the calling and purpose that God has given us and not someone else's. We don't have the grace for another person's purpose. We don't have the anointing for another person's purpose. When we remember this, it will help us to remain aligned with *the good, acceptable, and perfect will of God (Romans 12).*

How our Savior Jesus Christ remained aligned with God's purpose was to remember God's will over His fleshly will. When Jesus asked God, if you can take this cup from me, not my will but your will be done. When he told Peter, "Get thee behind me Satan, because you are an offence to me, you do not want the things of God but that of men (Matthew 16:23)," He was sticking with the purpose and will of God for His life.

Dying on the cross, being crucified, buried, resurrected, and ascending into heaven may not have seemed like a good thing to men, but it certainly was a good thing to God! God saw this as good because He wanted to save us, "mankind," from an eternal curse that would have stuck to us after Adam and Eve sinned in the garden. God's plan for our redemption served a "greater purpose" than Jesus remaining in the earth as a fleshly man. His plan transcended humanity. His purpose for Jesus Christ even gave us the opportunity to be filled with the Holy Spirit, which is the spirit of Jesus Christ!

I love how God continues to show us, that *His thoughts are as the heavens are higher from the earth, so are his ways higher than our thoughts and his ways are higher than our ways (Isaiah 55:9).*

Never approach your purpose with a know-it-all perspective. Your purpose is greater than you! It isn't even about you! Your purpose is about God and His plans.

Prayer:

Heavenly Father, I thank you for what you are doing in my life. I thank you for placing your purpose inside of me. As I submit my will to your will, I ask that you help me to understand the breadth, length, depth, and height of the love of Jesus Christ that passes knowledge, so that I might be filled with all the fullness of God. Father, I thank you for establishing your plans in my life and for fulfilling your purpose and will in Jesus' name. Amen.

CHAPTER 5

Grace for Your Purpose

RACE IS A GIFT from God that has been given to us. It is the Greek word *"Charis,"* in the "Strong's Concordance," reference #G5485. Grace is defined as: good will, loving-kindness, favor, the merciful kindness by which God, exerting his holy influence upon souls, turns them to Christ, keeps, strengthens, increases them in Christian faith, knowledge, affection and kindles them to exercise of the Christian virtues.

Ephesians 4:7 says, "But unto every one of us is given grace according to the measure of the gift of Christ." This means that the gift that was given to you by Jesus Christ, comes with the grace to operate in it.

But why would we need grace for our gift? We need grace (the merciful kindness of God) so that we can operate in the measure of the gift that was given to us by God, so that we will be able to fulfill His purpose in our lives.

God's grace keeps us as we maneuver in our purpose. As believers *we walk by faith, and not by sight (2 Corinthians 5:7),* so we must believe that we can do what we have been called to do. If we are intercessors, we must believe that our gift of intercession is working because it is God who causes our prayers to be answered. If we prophesy, we must believe that what God uses us to say will come to pass because He said it. We must be sure of God.

This doesn't mean that you won't doubt. That's why you have faith, so that your gift will be developed. No baby comes out of the womb walking, talking, eating formed food, or being able to follow instructions. You will make mistakes while learning and operating in your purpose. You will get discouraged, want to quit, feel ineffective, feel like what you're doing does not matter or even that people don't recognize the greatness of your gift. This is when grace comes in.

The definition of grace tells us that it keeps us, strengthens, increases our Christian faith, knowledge, affection, and kindles us to exercise of the Christian virtues. Isn't that amazing. It sounds like "Grace" keeps us intact as believers as we walk in our calling and purpose.

I also believe that God gives us grace so that we can fulfill His purpose in our lives. The Bible tells us: *that the gifts and callings of God are without repentance (Romans 11:29).* This is God's covenant with His children. We are God's children. God doesn't regret giving you a gift, calling, or purpose. He delights in your assignment, your gifts, callings, and purpose! He has your back one hundred percent.

This gives us confidence in God that He can perform His will in us and through our lives. I am immediately taken to *Philippians 1:6,* that he

that has begun a work in you, is faithful to perform it until the day of Jesus Christ! We must
believe that we will fulfill God's purpose, that
the gift He has given us is real, and that we have
been GRACED to do it! How amazing is that?

When you want to quit, throw in the towel,
draw back, or dumb down, remember that God
has graced you, and it is His will for you to operate in the Gifts that He has given you and fulfill
His purpose.

Prayer:

Heavenly Father, I thank you for the grace
that you have bestowed upon my life, in order
for me to fulfill your purpose and to do your
will. Lord, thank you that I am able to acknowledge that you are the giver of life, and peace.
Thank you for giving me peace as I endeavor to
fulfill your purpose, knowing that because you
started this work in me, that it will be performed
because you are the author and finisher of my
faith. In Jesus' name. Amen.

CHAPTER 6

Staying Connected To The Vine

WE MUST REMAIN CONNECT-ED to the source of our purpose, which is Jesus Christ, our Lord and Savior. The Apostle James tells us that *"whatever is good and perfect is a gift coming down to us from God our Father, who created all the lights in heavens" (James 1:17 NLT)*. This is why we must remain connected to the source!

If we are not connected to the Lord as we walk in our purpose, we won't be fruitful. The Lord doesn't get any glory in us not being fruitful. This is found in John chapter 15. Before we

delve into those scriptures, I want you to remember when Jesus walked by the fig tree and
cursed it because it didn't have any figs on it.

Jesus cursed the tree because it didn't produce figs when it was supposed to be fruitful.
It only had leaves on it. This brought Jesus no
glory. He couldn't eat from the fig tree when he
was hungry *(Matthew 21:18-19)*. The Kingdom
of God is created to prosper from the fruit of the
believers. Because God is fruitful, He expects us
to be fruitful and the only way we will remain
fruitful is by staying connected to the Vine.

Jesus Christ is the vine. He makes that clear
for us in *John chapter 15*. God the Father takes
care of the "Vine." A Vine dresser is a person
who prunes, trains, and cultivates vines. This is
what God does for us. We are connected to Jesus
Christ, and He is the vine; we are an extension
of him. We are only the branches when we stay
connected to Him, so we will be fruitful as God
the Father prunes, trains, and cultivates us.

The purpose of remaining connected to the
vine is so that we can grow continually to be

the beautiful tree that God has called us to in the Kingdom of God. The Bible tells us that the Kingdom of God is like a tree that was planted with a mustard seed (very small) and grew to be the biggest tree and the birds of the air came and made their nests in its branches *(Luke 13:18)*.

As we stay connected to the "Vine" Jesus Christ, we will be fruitful and continue to walk in the purpose that God has set for us. We won't get off track. We won't do things to make the kingdom of God look ineffective. We will be proficient and walk in excellence as we are being purposeful.

God delights in us being fruitful. He delights in being able to prune us because our branches have produced so much fruit that we need to be beautified again. If you watch a tree when it is going through the necessary seasons. It looks different in every season. No two seasons are alike for the tree or its branches. Even the leaves look different. They even fall off. The branches may break off at some point, but they eventually grow back out. The branches bud and the fruit is produced. Then, it is time to reap the harvest from the fruit so that it is consumed and does not go to waste.

When we are walking in our purpose, the fruit that we produce is given to God. The fruit may be bringing people into the Kingdom of God through salvation, helping to increase the faith of other believers, ministering deliverance to believers, operating in the gift of healing others, whether spiritually or physically, and so on. We must remain connected to the Vine so that we are producing the right fruit.

What happens when we don't remain connected to the vine? We don't bear fruit. We can do nothing. We're thrown away like a branch and wither, gathered, thrown into the fire, and burned. This is not God's desire for us or Jesus Christ, our Lord and Savior.

Prayer:

Heavenly Father, If I am not connected to your Son Jesus Christ as the Vine, I pray that I am reconnected. I pray that you will help me to abide in the Word of God, so that the Word of God will abide in me. I want to be fruitful in every area of my life, so that you will have the glory and honor. I want you to be fully pleased with me. Thank you for your love and for helping me to do your will and fulfill your purpose. In Jesus' name. Amen.

CHAPTER 7

Discerning Times and Seasons

CCLESIASTES 3:1 SAYS, *"To everything there is a season, and a time to every purpose under heaven"*

God's divine timing is significant to your purpose in life. Being out of alignment with the timing and seasons of the Lord can produce frustration, make you feel inept, and uncapable of operating in your purpose.

Reading the excerpt of scriptures in *Ecclesiastes 3:1-8* helps you to understand that there is a purpose in everything and the seasons of our lives. We go through different seasons of our lives, and we must do things in those seasons. As we continue to mature and age, we may operate in a specific purpose in one season and not others or vice versa.

Compromise

Compromise is a strategy of the enemy to get us out of the divine timing of the Lord. If he can get you to take a different route than what God has instructed for you to take, he will cause you to be off track with your assignment and purpose. The Bible says in *Psalms 37:23 NLT,* *"The LORD directs the steps of the godly. He delights in every detail of their lives."*

Seeking the Lord

We must seek the Lord as we walk in our purpose, so that we will know what we should be doing in every season. We simply ask the Lord, "Father, what is that you want me to do right now?" Sometimes the Lord will instruct you to "Rest." Rest is a preparation and a strategy that the Lord uses so that you are prepared for what is next as you walk in His purpose.

When we seek the Lord for direction, it pleases God because what we are saying to Him is "I need you." "I can't do this without you." "I need your help."

God is:
- **Omniscient** – All-Knowing God
- **Omnipotent** – All Powerful God. His power is unlimited and he is able to do anything.
- **Omnipresent** – All Present God. He is everywhere at the same time.

Because of this, we can rest assured that we will prosper and fulfill the purpose of God in our lives as we seek Him for guidance, rely on His infinite wisdom, and trust His directions. We must be okay with the guidance that God gives us, the people He sends into our lives as divine helpers and the outcome.

Being Led by The Spirit of God

When Elijah ran from Jezebel in *1 Kings 19,* he was encountered by the "Angel of the Lord." *The angel instructed him to eat and drink and allowed him to sleep because the journey ahead would be too great for him (1 Kings 19:4-8).* Because of Elijah's obedience to the Angel of the Lord, he was able to travel for forty days and forty nights. That is amazing. If Elijah wasn't obedient, he would have perished on his way to the destination.

Jesus Christ was "led" into the wilderness by the Holy Spirit to be tempted by the devil and fasted forty days and forty nights. If he would have gone into the wilderness to fast and be tempted by the devil without being "led" by the Holy Spirit, He would not have endured and fulfilled His purpose. Jesus overcame every temptation that is common to man after He fasted. He had to overcome, so that we could overcome. His obedience to the Spirit of God, catapulted Him into His ministry and completion of His purpose.

The Bible tells us in *Romans 8:14,* "*As many as are led by the Spirit of God, they are the sons of*

God." When we allow the Lord to lead and guide us, we are called "sons of God." I want to always be called a son of God.

This doesn't mean that you won't get it wrong, or make a mistake. It just means that you are seeking the Lord and attempting to be obedient to Him. Sometimes the enemy will try to confuse you with his voice, which is a voice of deception.

The Bible warns and tells us that, *"my sheep hear my voice and the voice of a stranger he will not follow, because they don't recognize his voice" (John 10:4-5 NIV).* The enemy will try to imitate the voice of God, but it won't align fully with the scriptures, what is written in the Word of God, or the initial instructions the Lord gave you.

Being prayerful is the key to hearing and discerning the Lord's voice over any other voice. The Bible tells us, *"Not to worry about anything; instead pray about everything. Tell God what you need and thank him for all he has done" (Philippians 4:6 NLT).*

Jesus never worried about fulfilling the purpose of God. He prayed that he *"Would"* fulfill the purpose of God. In the garden of Gethsemane, he prayed three times to God, *"if you would take this cup from me, nevertheless, not my will (purpose), but your will (purpose) be done!"* (Matthew 26:39).

Jesus knew what God's purpose was and stated this many times to prepare his disciples and the multitudes for it. His disciples were not pleased with His purpose. The multitudes became offended at His purpose. However, this didn't change Jesus's perspective or cause Him to reject His purpose.

The Purpose of Jesus Christ:

- The Savior of God's people *(Matthew 1:21)*
- God with us *(Matthew 1:23)*
- The Governor to rule the people of Israel *(Matthew 1:6)*
- The government of God to rest upon his shoulder, the Wonderful Counselor,

Mighty God, Prince of Peace, and Ever-lasting Father *(Isaiah 9:6)*

- His government and peace to be never ending, upon the throne of David, and upon His kingdom to order it and to establish it with judgment and justice forever *(Isaiah 9:7)*
- Reign over the house of Jacob forever *(Luke 1:33)*
- To understand our infirmities and temptations *(Hebrews 4:15)*
- Allow us to enter behind the veil *(Hebrews 10:19)*
- The Author of Eternal Salvation *(Hebrews 5:9)*
- Be our High Priest *(Hebrews 5:10)*
- Be the surety of a better testament *(Hebrews 7:22)*
- To seek and save the lost *(Luke 19:10)*
- To destroy the works of the enemy *(1 John 3:8)*
- To fulfill the law *(Matthew 5:17)*
- To open blind eyes, open deaf ears, cause the lame to walk, lepers cleansed, dead raised, poor receive the gospel, cast out demons *(Luke 7:22)*

- The true light that lights every man that enters the world *(John 1:9)*
- That we should have eternal life and not perish *(John 3:15)*
- Become the end of the law for righteousness for those who believe in Him *(Romans 10:4)*
- The Shepherd and Bishop (overseer of our souls)

These are just a few of His purpose. There is so much more; as we study the word of God, we will understand more.

Prayer:

Heavenly Father, I ask that you help me understand and know my times and seasons, just like the sons of Issachar. Lord help me to always be in alignment with what you are calling me to complete in your perfect timing. I trust your timing and your plans. Let me be led by your Holy Spirit every day. In Jesus' name. Amen.

I pray that this book enlightened your understanding concerning purpose. I pray that as you continue to walk in the Lord, follow him, and pursue his purpose for your life, that you can discern your times and seasons. That you will know what to do, where to go, who to make connections with and that you have a greater understanding of your purpose. I pray as the Holy Spirit helps you to discern your times and seasons, that you will be obedient as you are being led by Him. I pray that the Lord will continue to be a lamp unto your feet and a light unto your path in Jesus' name. Amen.

About The Author

NIKEYA QUICK HAS THREE wonderful sons. She is a woman of faith and an author. Her endless pursuit of Jesus Christ and her heart for God helps her complete the assignment on her life.

Her passion for the new believer and those who are backslidden are consistent with the word of God. She ministers salvation to those who are lost while she shops, attends events, and by the leading of the Holy Spirit in certain areas of her region.

She is a partner at a Bible-Based ministry in Charlotte, NC, and is accountable to her leaders.

She is an encourager to others and will intercede for them to see them fulfill the purpose and destiny God created for them. Her utmost desire is to see the body of Christ in unity, as it speaks of in *Ephesians 4:1-13*.

She is also the author of the following books:
- Walking Into Your Destiny By Faith
- Zeal Without Knowledge

References

1. J. Suttie (2020). The Greater Good Science Center at the University of California, Berkeley. Seven Ways to Find Your Purpose in Life.

2. https://greatergood.berkeley.edu/article/item/seven_ways_to_find_your_purpose_in_life

3. Oxford University Press (2023). Oxford English Dictionary. OED

4. https://www.oed.com/search/dictionary/?scope=Entries&q=purpose

Index

A

accusations, 12, 15

Adam, 27

administrator, 3

adolescence, 19

adversity, 12

affection, 29, 31

Angel, 41

Apostle James, 33

apostles, 19, 20

ascension, 16

assignment, 15, 31, 39, 47

aunt, 3

author, 32, 47, 48

B

bear, 25, 36

Beelzebub, 12

believer, 4, 47

betrayal, 12, 15

Bible, 7, 13, 21, 24, 31, 35, 39, 41, 42, 47

biblical views, 4

Bishop, 45

body of Christ, 20, 48

branches, 34, 35

bread, 12

brother, 15

burial, 16

C

Charlotte, 47

childhood, 3

Christian, 29, 31

church, 20

comfort, 21

commandments, 14

compassion, 4

competition, 21

Compromise, 39

corn, 14

covetousness, 21

creation, 6

creator, 9

cross, 15, 27

crown of thorns, 15

crucifixion, 16

curse, 27

D

daughter, 3

death, 15, 16

deception, 42

demons, 14, 16, 44

destination, 41

Destiny, 48

devil, 12, 13, 14, 41

direction, 40

disappointed, 2

discern, 46

disciples, 11, 14, 15, 43

discouraged, 11, 31

disobedience, 25

dominion, 6, 8, 9

doubt, 30

dove, 11

E

earth, 2, 4, 6, 7, 8, 9, 13, 16, 22, 27
edify, 19
Elijah, 41
emotions, 2
empty, 2
encourager, 4, 48
enemy, 39, 42, 44
envy, 12, 21
evangelists, 19
evangelize, 3
Eve, 27
events, 47
evil, 24
exaltation, 21
exercise, 29, 31
exhortation, 21

F

failure, 1
faith, 4, 21, 22, 29, 30, 31, 32, 36, 47
Faith, 20, 48
family, 4

Father, 15, 28, 33, 34, 39, 44

favor, 29

female, 7

figs, 34

friend, 3

fruitful, 7, 9, 33, 34, 35, 37

frustrated, 11

frustration, 38

G

Gethsemane, 15, 43

giftings, 19, 21, 22

glory, 4, 9, 19, 22, 33, 34, 37

God, 2, 4, 6, 7, 8, 9, 10, 11, 12, 13, 14, 15, 16, 17, 18, 19, 20, 21, 22, 23, 24, 25, 26, 27, 28, 29, 30, 31, 32, 33, 34, 35, 36, 37, 38, 39, 40, 41, 42, 43, 44, 45, 47, 48

good, 2, 18, 20, 24, 25, 26, 27, 29, 33

Gospel, 10

governments, 20

Governor, 43

grace, 1, 13, 14, 26, 29, 30, 31, 32

gratitude, 2

guidance, 40

H

Happiness, 2
harvest, 35
haters, 11
heart, 9, 14, 25, 47
heaven, 19, 27, 38
Heavenly Father, 4, 9, 16, 22, 28, 32, 36, 45
hero, 12
hierarchy, 20, 21
High Priest, 44
high priests, 22
High Priests, 13
high school, 3
Holy Spirit, 11, 27, 41, 45, 46, 47
honor, 37
hope, 11
hopeless, 1
human beings, 1, 7, 8
humanity, 8, 10, 13, 16, 19, 27

I

infirmities, 44
intercessor, 3, 16
intercessors, 30

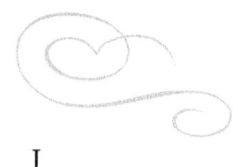

J

jealousy, 12, 21
Jeremiah, 17, 18, 24
Jesse, 25
Jesus Christ, 3, 4, 10, 11, 13, 15, 16, 26, 27, 28, 30, 32, 33, 34, 35, 36, 41, 43, 47
John the Baptist, 11

K

kindness, 4, 29, 30
King David, 24
Kingdom of God, 35, 36
kingdoms, 13
knowledge, 3, 20, 28, 29, 31
Knowledge, 48

L

law, 13, 14, 44, 45
leader, 3, 25
lepers, 44
lies, 12

life, 1, 3, 4, 5, 8, 9, 10, 13, 14, 16, 18, 24, 26, 27, 28, 32, 37, 38, 45, 46, 47

lion, 25

Lord, 7, 8, 9, 14, 16, 18, 20, 21, 22, 25, 26, 32, 33, 36, 38, 39, 40, 41, 42, 45, 46

love, 7, 10, 27, 28, 37

Love, 14

M

male, 7

minister, 4, 15

ministry, 4, 11, 19, 41, 47

miracles, 14, 20, 21

mistakes, 30

mockery, 12

mother, 3, 15, 17, 23

mustard seed, 35

N

neighbor, 14

New Testament, 24

O

obedience, 12, 41

obstacles, 4

Old Testament, 24

Omnipotent, 40

Omnipresent, 40

Omniscient, 40

opposition, 11

P

pastors, 19

Paul, 20

peace, 32, 44

people, 3, 7, 11, 13, 14, 15, 21, 24, 25, 31, 36, 40, 43

persecution, 12

Peter, 26

Pharisees, 13, 22

plans, 27, 28, 45

pleasure, 18

praise dancer, 3

pray, 4, 9, 16, 36, 42, 45, 46

prayers, 30

Prince of Peace, 44

Prophecy, 21

prophesy, 21, 30

prophets, 14, 19, 20

purpose, 1, 2, 3, 4, 7, 8, 9, 10, 11, 12, 13, 15, 16, 17, 18, 19, 21, 22, 23, 24, 26, 27, 28, 30, 31, 32, 33, 34, 35, 36, 37, 38, 39, 40, 41, 43, 45, 46, 48

R

religious leaders, 13

repentance, 31

Rest, 39

resurrection, 16

righteousness, 24, 45

S

sabbath, 14

Sadducees, 13, 22

salvation, 3, 4, 36, 47

Samuel, 25

Savior, 26, 33, 36, 43

scribes, 22

Scribes, 13

scriptures, 9, 34, 38, 42

seasons, 35, 38, 39, 45, 46

sheep, 24, 25, 42

Shepherd, 24, 45

shepherd boy, 24

sins, 16

sister, 3, 15

slogans, 11

social media, 3

sons of Issachar, 45

soul, 14

surrender, 5

T

talents, 2, 18, 19

teachers, 19, 20

temptation, 12, 41

thoughts, 11, 24, 27

tongues, 20, 21

U

unity, 48

V

victim mentality, 11

video, 3

Vine, 33, 34, 35, 36

voice, 42

W

wife, 3
wilderness, 12, 41
wisdom, 20, 40
womb, 17, 23, 30
Word, 10, 12, 13, 18, 20, 21, 22, 23, 36, 42
worship, 13

Z

Zeal, 48

PURPOSEFUL

www.ingramcontent.com/pod-product-compliance
Lightning Source LLC
Chambersburg PA
CBHW070933120626
46546CB00004B/1407